Daryl Cagle's "Rich, Greedy, Crooked WALL STREET" Coloring Book!
Artwork and text by Daryl Cagle

Published by Cagle Cartoons, Inc.
ISBN-13: 978-0692706626
ISBN-10: 0692706623
Printed in the United States of America, First Printing: May, 2016

Sucking the Blood out of the Economy

Our bullish economy races a bit more slowly as the wealthy one percent bleeds us all dry.

EXECUTIVE GREED

DARYL CAGLE

Executive Golden Parachutes

The economy crashes, businesses fall flat, but greedy executives fill their pockets for a soft landing. The 99% can only watch, and complain.

DARYL CAGLE

Goldman Sachs and their "Muppets"

At the giant Wall Street investment bank Goldman Sachs, investors were called "Muppets" because they would do what they were told, including buying worthless mortgage backed securities.

President Obama and Wall Street

Obama inherited the Wall Street collapse, but despite obvious, widespread fraud that raped the economy, the Obama administration never sent a Wall Street executive to jail and hired top Wall Street executives for top positions in the government.

Obama Rushes in to Put Out the Fire

As banks cheated investors and Wall Street executives continued to pay themselves massive bonuses despite their failures, President Obama's solution was to throw more money at the banks because they were "too big to fail."

Deep Roots in Washington

The roots of our financial troubles are in Washington where politicians are stuck in place.

Wall Street Money Moves Congress

Greedy Wall Street has learned that dangling money in front of politicians gets them where they want to go.

Our Sick Economy

Washington politicians argue as we suffer.

DARYL
CAGLE

Politicians in Wall Street's Pockets

Even as Washington politicians decry Wall Street greed, they do Wall Street's bidding.

Pensions Crushed

States across America are facing huge budget crises as pension funds can't meet their obligations. Republicans blame unions rather than Wall Street.

The Wall Street Journal Joins the Fox News Family

The parent company of Republican champion Fox News purchased the venerable Wall Street Journal.

China Consumes Dollars

China continued to gobble up many billions of dollars in the form of financing America's growing debt.

DARYL CAGLE

China Pounds the Dollar

China's artificially low exchange rates keep Chinese goods cheap and give the American economy a pounding.

DARYL CAGLE

Occupy Wall Street

The "Occupy Wall Street" protesters often waved this cartoon that illustrated how they were viewed by Wall Street.

Fox News and Occupy Wall Street

The Occupy Wall Street protesters were portrayed as fools on Fox News, which often picked the least articulate spokesmen to interview.

Fox News and Gold

The Fox News Channel is filled with advertisements pushing gold as an investment for worried, elderly Americans who fear an economic collapse.

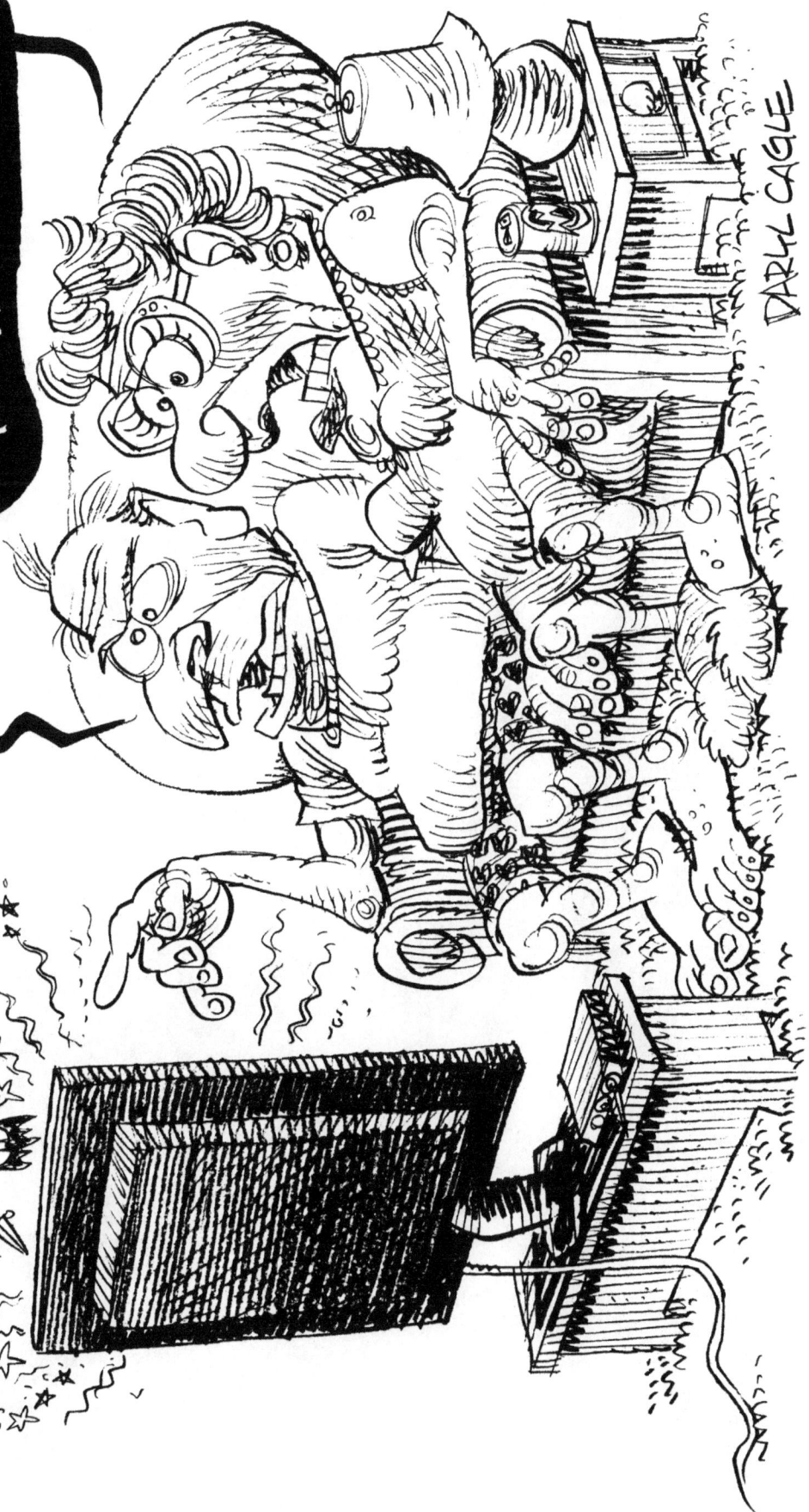

The Mortgage Crisis Comes Back to Bite Wall Street

Wall Street's mortgage Ponzi scheme came back to bite them in 2008 – no matter, an economic collapse wasn't enough to hurt executive bonuses as Wall Street was bailed out by Washington.

Mortgage Lemmings

America was beset by foreclosures as falling real estate values caused millions of Americans to lose their homes, caused by Wall Street's fraudulent mortgage securities.

DARYL CAGLE MSNBC.com

Anyone Qualifies for a Mortgage

Crooked banks sold mortgages to millions of Americans who should never have qualified for the mortgages and could not pay back the loans.

The Stock Market Fell by 50%

Although Washington and Wall Street were responsible for the crash, it seemed there was no one to blame.

Federal Reserve Chairwoman Janet Yellen

Wall Street jumps at every statement that comes out of the Federal Reserve.

Oil Prices Drag Down Wall Street

Whenever the price of oil falls, so does the stock market.

Economic Fears

The economic world is a frightening place.

Money Talks

In their "Citizens United" decision, the Supreme Court opened the doors to massive political spending by rich corporations.

Free Speech.

More Free Speech.

We Look Up to Wall Street

... and Wall Street looks down on us.

WALL STREET

DARYL CAGLE

For the past 35 years, Daryl Cagle has been one of America's most prolific cartoonists. He worked for 15 years with Jim Henson's Muppets, illustrating scores of books, magazines, calendars, and all manner of products. Daryl still sees pigs, frogs, Sesame Street and Fraggle Rock characters when he closes his eyes. He worked as the editorial cartoonist in Hawaii, then was the cartoonist for the Washington Post's Slate.com site and msnbc.com. Daryl is America's most widely syndicated editorial cartoonist.

To see more of Daryl's work visit DarylCagle.com. To reprint cartoons from Daryl and from the top editorial cartoonists around the world, visit PoliticalCartoons.com or call (805) 969-2829.

Collect All of the Daryl Cagle Coloring Books at CagleBook.com

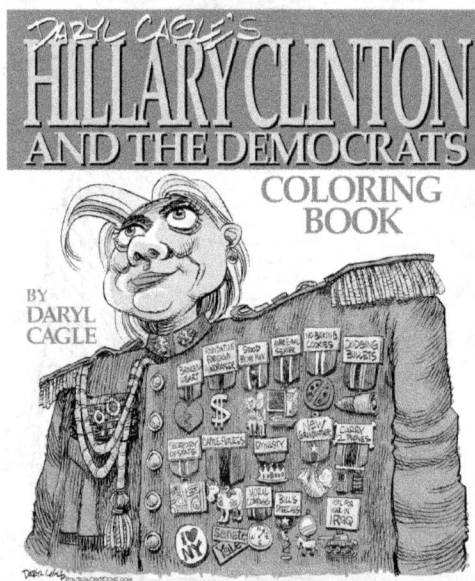

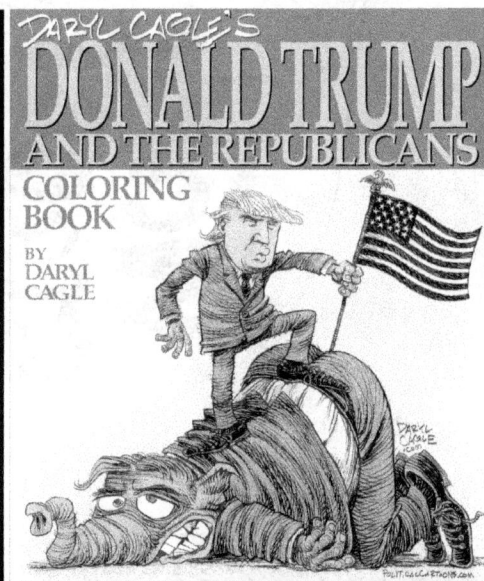

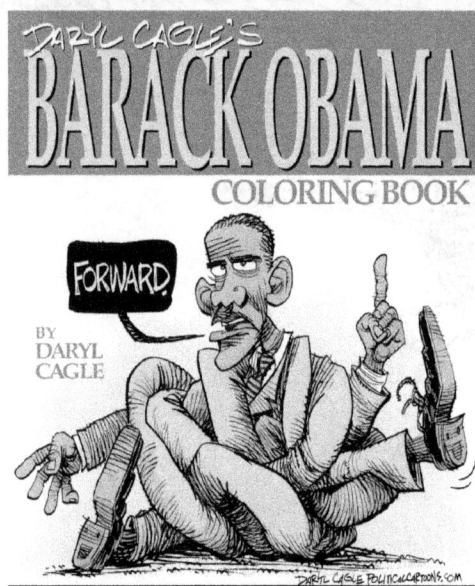

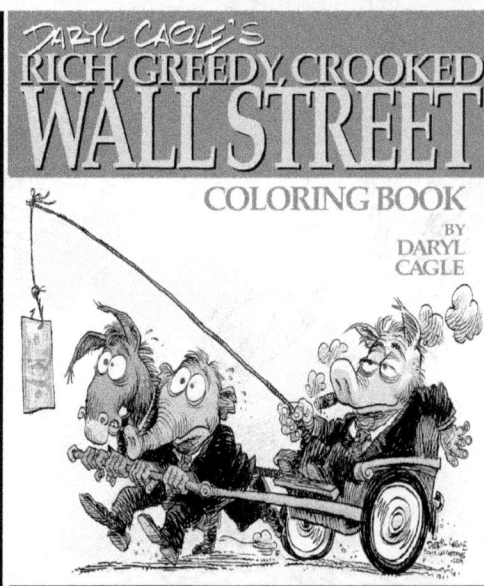

DARYL CAGLE'S HILLARY CLINTON AND THE DEMOCRATS COLORING BOOK BY DARYL CAGLE

DARYL CAGLE'S DONALD TRUMP AND THE REPUBLICANS COLORING BOOK BY DARYL CAGLE

DARYL CAGLE'S BARACK OBAMA COLORING BOOK BY DARYL CAGLE

DARYL CAGLE'S RICH, GREEDY, CROOKED WALL STREET COLORING BOOK BY DARYL CAGLE